The Wind Softly Murmurs
Poems of Family Love and Loss

By

Sharon Arthur

Hourglass Island Press
Williamsburg, Virginia

The Wind Softly Murmurs
Poems of Family Love and Loss

© 2019 by Sharon Arthur

All rights reserved. This book or any portion thereof may not be reproduced or used in any manner whatsoever without the express, written permission of the publisher except for the use of brief quotations in a book review.

Printed in the United States of America

First Printing 2019
ISBN: 978-1-732205604
LCCN: 2018945270

Hourglass Island Press
36 Priorslee Lane
Williamsburg, VA 23185

Publisher's Cataloging-In-Publication Data
(Prepared by The Donohue Group, Inc.)

Names: Arthur, Sharon (Sharon T.), 1956-
Title: The wind softly murmurs : poems of family love and loss / by Sharon Arthur.
Description: Williamsburg, VA : Hourglass Island Press [2019]
Identifiers: ISBN 9781732205604 | ISBN 9781732205611 (ebook)
Subjects: LCSH: Grief--Poetry. | Parents--Death--Psychological aspects—Poetry. | Families--Poetry. | Spiritual healing--Poetry. | LCGFT: Poetry. | BISAC: POETRY / Subjects & Themes / Death, Grief, Loss. | FAMILY & RELATIONSHIPS / Death, Grief, Bereavement. | SELF-HELP / Death, Grief, Bereavement.
Classification: LCC PS3601.R764 W56 2019 (print) | LCC PS3601.R764 (ebook) | DDC 811/.6--dc23

Dedication

In Memoriam,
I dedicate this book to my beloved father
who directs my hand
in writing these poems and guides my heart
wherever it roams.

Always, Love Sharon

Acknowledgments

With love and gratitude to my father, Eric Arthur, who, in life, shared with me his beautiful soul and love, which continues on even in death. You are my writing partner and muse of inspiration for these poems.

With love and gratitude to my mother, Mildred Arthur, whose warmth and love still surround me from the other side. You are helping me to become a better writer.

For my sister, Julie Arthur, whose patient sacrifices for this book supported and encouraged me. You helped make it possible. Thanks for being there for me and believing in me when I needed it.

My deepest gratitude and thanks go to Kym McBride, who has been all things to me: my spiritual counselor, teacher, mentor, life coach, writing coach, book shepherd, and technical computer aid. This book couldn't have happened without your help. Thanks for believing in me and the dream and for never giving up on me, even when I wanted to. You have transformed who I am with your caring and friendship.

Ron Frazer was my editor, formatter, and cover designer on this book. He went above and beyond to help with virtually every other aspect of the publishing process, from producing the book, to getting it to press, and printing it. The extra time you gave me on this project has helped make it possible, and your efforts to make it a success are greatly appreciated.

My many thanks and appreciation also go to Mary Grodek for her editing services, editorial advice, and input on this book. I am grateful for your support and belief in the work. Your assistance has helped make the book possible.

My thanks also go to George Lechter from Technology Alternatives Corp. for modifying my computer equipment to meet my special needs. Without your help I would still be struggling to get the poems on paper. Today's modern typewriter is the computer, so I am grateful that due to your professional skills, you were able to make the necessary changes.

Table of Contents

Dedication

Acknowledgments

Introduction

Chapter One. 1

  Death and Loss

      The Body 3
      On Facing Death 5
      The Mirror 9
      The Dust 13
      Death 15
      The Spider .17
      Death's Airs 19
      Confusion 21
      Alone 25
      The Crowd .29
      The Memorial 33

Chapter Two 39

  Family Love and Memories

      For My Father 41
      My Father's Jacket 45
      Mother's Birthday Memorial 47
      Grief 51
      The Stage 53
      A Mother's Love 57

The Begotten. 61
The Brow 63
The Gift 67
Cut from the Same Cloth 69

Chapter Three 73
Eternal Life and Renewal

Identity Search. 75
The Physique. 77
The Moss 79
Resurrection 81
The Bones 85
Persistence 87
The Colors of Time. .89
Transformation 93
Immortality. 95

AUTHOR BIOGRAPHY

Introduction

These poems represent my emotional journey that began with the loss of my parents. After I had processed some of my grief from the deaths of my father in 2006 and my mother in 2014, my feelings flooded onto paper in these poems. I have found great transformational catharsis in pouring my emotions into these writings.

The poems tell a mystical, lyrical story about my experiences. It follows in a line from start to finish, culminating in an uplifting conclusion that I hope will bring peace and nourishment to your soul in your bereavement.

The book begins with the physical death of my parents, continues with thoughts of aging, and the regret that stems from the recognition that all matter deteriorates over time. It goes into several topics: the helplessness we feel over our fate being woven long before we are born, and the confusion and loneliness brought about by the loss of loved ones. While the poems explore souls and spirits, and the inevitability that all bodily flesh will die, they remind us that love remains and endures eternally. The book encourages us to know that our ancestors await us on the other side.

The second chapter moves into childhood memories of my parent's love, the values and ideals they taught me, and the beauty in the world that they encouraged me to enjoy. They gave me a family heritage that continues as a gift to me. It includes an appreciation of beauty, truth, and love. Such intangibles are the greatest gift of all. No inheritance of physical objects can ever match such a divine, spiritual legacy. This chapter ends with family karma—that the characteristics of our loved ones live on in us. This is a thought that may bring us some consolation.

The final chapter explores several themes that center on our personal relationship to time and place. The poems suggest that we can discover our current identity by looking to the past—to our ancestors to see who they were. The poems examine the idea that you can't know where you're going unless you know where you've been. Our physical bodies come from the earth and return to it eventually—ashes to ashes, dust to dust. While it is true that in time we lose all our physicality, there is a physical rebirth from the earth; life is renewed every year in the spring as part of the never-ending cycle of life and of the seasons. It gives us solace and strength here on earth to continue on. The poems then move into more metaphysical realms to revisit the topics of ancestors, the past, evolution, transformation, and finally the afterlife and the eternal life of the soul. Interwoven throughout the book are repeated themes of the soul, eternal life, and renewal.

The message of the book tells us not to get trapped in the past, but persist in moving forward into the future on our life's journey. In the early years of my grief, I found that I wanted to suspend time, stop it, return to my childhood and renew the beauty of the earlier seasons of my life as they were, but I was unable to. During my grief I didn't want anything to ever change, for all to remain the same. But change comes regardless, relentlessly, and can't be resisted. Eventually it leads to evolution and new life, a positive thing.

These poems reflect my belief that no one ever really dies. The physical flesh we inhabit is temporal. We are not our bodies, we are souls that inhabit a body for only a short time. Our souls, not temporal but eternal, survive independently of our bodies. I also believe that we have many rebirths. We have rebirths during our physical lifetime here on earth, where a new life is always possible for us if we can let go of the past and accept change. We have rebirths in metaphysical terms, in our soul's eternal life where we still continue to learn and grow even on the other side, moving ever closer to perfection.

I am bringing my poems to you, my readers, in the desire that these heartfelt works may help those of you who, like myself, are grieving, and traveling on your own journey through love and loss. I hope that you will find some comfort here. Perhaps these poems will cause you to contemplate your own lives and experiences and think about them in a deeper or different way.

We will all experience loss in our lives if we live long enough. It's not about whether it hurts, because it always does. It's what we do with that pain that makes a life worthy of living.

> Sharon Arthur
> September 5, 2018

Chapter One
Death and Loss

The Body

This hourglass body stiffens
it cannot move limbs but flies like griffins
into the oxygen at night
a canister of joyful height

lifts up the apparition
leaving an imprint on the sheets in a fission
splitting in two her atoms bred
where her frame lay on the bed

this lioness born with golden wings
glides in the air, comets swirl in rings
around her orbs of sifting sand
finally sets on her finger's wedding band

a union in a haven of fire

physique consumed by death's desire

her gaze drained by fluid's dissolution

ever devolved to a ghostly solution

though oblivious on a pad she lays

sounds a prayer for better days

still the dainty slipper chimes her footfall on the stairs

a glass is raised, we toast a life of no more cares.

On Facing Death

Eyes wide open that stare a thoughtless word
as the priest reads the bible, the crowd is stirred
on the judgement day is granted absolution
when confession reaches man's solution

your body rises in the moonless night
high over mountain where hermits are granted sight
in caves their prayers are seen
by a second-sighted high priestess queen

she dances with fairies on your grave
the wake proceeds in the church's nave
the cross and candles speak the pulpit's tongue
as the mourners' chorus is sorrowfully sung

loved by Aphrodite with votive flames in jars
your portrait painted eloquently by the stars
fate is a cross stitch woven loosely on the loom
by a spider whose body we exhume

into a monument your epitaph is written
all of life was a glory you had bitten
the holy grail is a search through man's blood
the fountain of youth is history's rosebud

as the nymphs will do a jig on your stone
hoping you led a life they can condone
green grass on you is their apparel
as they drink the wine from the nearest barrel

you could not face this death lying in your tomb
so you hid your creation far in the whale's womb
she rises to the surface for a shallow breath of air
on Charon's boat at him you stare

from the River Styx he ascends
commencing your new life in a form he amends
this mighty spectral shadow haunts your dreams
as you see the spider's web in daylight sunbeams

comes the four horsemen of the apocalypse
in the hour of your birth's eclipse
overshadowing the moon's sweeping tide
as Pluto becomes your everlasting guide.

The Mirror

I saw your image you and I
in the mirror nearly walked by
you missed my past ambling toward my fate
I crossed your future traveling too late

we met briefly in the center but not long enough
for me to dab my nose with my powder puff
my face had lines that I never before perceived
only in the mirror was my age aggrieved

I spoke to you to affirm my existence
but you only replied with your superior consistence
your voice echoed as though through ancient stone
ringing in a cave before men turned to bone

I could not match your sylvan, sonorous voice
even though we were the identical name choice
for my past did not slide smoothly on skates
so easily through my future's closed gates

my every hair had turned stone grey
surely this imitation was leading me astray
while the years counted in this reproduction
as the original version I felt no destruction

my auburn comb had lost some teeth
when wet its dye ran underneath
my fingernails as I raked it through my strands
my hair tendrils curling through gossamer lands

apparitions seen only in the mirror
a reverse world coming closer, clearer
I raised my hand in a salutatory greeting
to my own copy in this region of meeting

you raised your hand to greet me back
but our hands could not touch,
                the glass was off track
cleaved in two by more than just steel
but a silvery other world that was more real

I said my world mattered as the only truth
you countered with only if I remained a youth
my flesh lines grew the more I appeared
like ancient tree bark by time seared

the dermis fell away in paper purveyors
revealing the actuality of my other worldly layers
my sheath like a corn husk was shucked from my
      frame
then I joined my twin in the mirror of my name.

The Dust

This speck of dust looks back at me
speaking a long soliloquy
of bygone times it can recall
on my mirror in the foyer's hall

these corridors of my discontent
are the dust layer's sad lament
reminding me how I began
a babe in arms to an adult who ran

fleeing the present, desiring to hide
in the dust only I can confide
I love the span this dust represents
like an old bookstore filled with musty scents

this earth reduced to tiny particles
on my furniture like magazine articles
that I read in my spare time
a fortune teller reading signs in mountain's lime

these dry bits of noteworthy news
are the substance of my poetic hues
revealing their story of how they were born
and the departed life that they now mourn

staring blankly in my face
scattered like a coverlet of lace
on the bureau it sits reminiscing
a gathered inscription to years I am missing.

Death

This absent state from which I draw no breath
this stillness in the cold starry night is a death
an ending of my joyous times
a closed book on my nursery rhymes

the nectar of the rose that bloomed
sweet fragrance pungent where I roomed
filling up my father's many homes
lived under life's turbulent domes

this life's closed and varied chapter,
becomes like dinosaurs, flying raptor
returns me to eons past
where I climb the rigging mast

of the ship from where my voyage sails
across the ocean's mighty vales
to the Isles where sibyls speak
and the nightingale moves its beak

to talk of forms to come
shadows are the earthly sum
added to the counting machine
of the corporeal that you can glean

this death has no width or size
just a finish line beyond which towers the prize
a quiz show that you have won
as the dial spins under fate's sun.

The Spider

The spider weaves man's tale of fate
with silken threads to bind the world
a tiny Hercules with strength unfurled
before we arrive at Hades' gate

a destiny strong holds us fast
prey caught in his net of gold
on a misty autumn morning cold
unseen by night in spaces vast

the patterns of our lives are visible alone
in sunlight's rays' illumination bright
caught at angles of vision's sight
as we turn up every stone

he spins his yarn in dark unseen
on giant looms where titans live
endless stories he will give
from the world that he can glean

the universe begins in his strong web
finality trapped in his lacy maze
upon his sustenance he fixes his gaze
to devour life at its flow and ebb

the spider sits upon a rock
writing in alphabets about his time
looking at stars as he spins in his prime
watching the old grandfather clock.

Death's Airs

On a winter's day entered death
into my body blew his icy breath
his taken form an ethereal carriage
in a search for perfect marriage

a towering shape stretching for miles
ends unsighted in catacomb's files
though a consort of angels banned from the flock
becomes the disguise of a priestly frock

the air he removes in a vacuum seal
is your sculpted clay he tries to steal
with frugal desires appear his gentle draught
poured into my blood from a teapot's spout

this distant land where he resides
a forbidding clime where no life hides
he arrives on the wind bearing gifts
I journey on seas of Elysian rifts

a life lived well speaks a heavenly abode
but if lightening divides the tree trunk's load
results in paradise islands swept
under ocean waves where seismic shifts are kept

once a somnolent island unto myself
now safely guarded on the celestial shelf
as the gales of life lash through the trees
the airs of death are the least of these.

Confusion

Blurring the lines
of harmony's signs
my role played
wind rising dismayed
whistled through trees
I thought was bees
humming a job
on their watch fob

I am confused
over goals used
recollections were mistaken
recycled bin taken
my colored room
painted in a bloom
of violet tulips
I saw as mint juleps

as breezes blustered
I became flustered
the eagle's cry
a formless lie
turns into linnets
in my mind's spinets
the piano plays
are my judgment's delays

a note sounds
as chaos abounds
echoes in skies
of indistinct ties
the warriors' lament
death's final advent
coming from where
thoughts that can tear

the universe forms
of mental storms
forges make lead
from Gorgon's head
clashing nebula swirl
turning into a pearl
skies are oceans
become my healing potions

corridors of abyss
are my bliss
my day's trauma
is life's comma
a pause mused
on bewildered wilderness fused
joins horizon's line
on my rising sign

stands of fir
live desert's myrrh
men from north
bring sands forth
comes wisdom's strain
against my progress's gain
experience then perplexed
is my memory hexed.

Alone

I stand upon the mountain top looking down from
    cirrus clouds
the only mortal amidst the wildflowers not dressed
    in nature's shrouds
no man nor beast beset me in these snowy tower
    passes
alone yet not forlorn
as the baby will be born
I emerge from the summit to join the masses

we glide into this world on a swiftly running brook
and exit in a painful season reading from the holy
    book
in and out we must steer without any aid
while the crowd joins our tour
this carnal drink we pour
before our silhouette at dusk will drowsily fade

sadness does not fall upon me as I walk with ghosts
they are my friends and show me my signposts
amidst the lofty cedars and sweet, sticky, scented
        pines
a forest of guileless options
in a sea of child adoptions
wrap around me like grape leaf vines

we cannot be alone if we walk with Greek Gods
searching for water with our divining rods
I drift through the foothills of my childhood dreams
a singular being singing
in harmony with trumpets ringing
as I stand in the sunlight's beams.

as I walk on the summit through these high plains'
	grasses
the burdens engulf me of being the lone one at the
	masses
for my cathedral no one else can enter
its pulpit is my speech
for the spirits within my reach
and it lies at the core of earth's molten center

I fear no evil from any human action
as a voice speaks volumes in gaining volcanic trac-
	tion
the crickets chirp softly outside my window pane
as night becomes early morn
and my heart is getting worn
I proceed alone in the drenching rain.

The Crowd

Late upon the midnight hours
when rises in darkness spirit's powers
as I lay my body to rest
in come many a welcome guest

walking through my dusky room
shades appearing in fated doom
filing past me numerous crowds
like the forms in fast-drifting clouds

moving by slowly, souls unknown
faces of angels in vapors wind blown
silent graphic figures passing
in sketchy outline they are amassing

features obscure in dim lit night
advancing through my corridor in their flight
discourse unspoken to my ears
I heed their lessons in my heart's tears

messages given on lonely paths
lives cleansed in sacred baths
as these forces wander through my mind
their presence haunts memories' places I find

as groups push into my space
shrinking increasingly into a tiny place
crowding me out of my sleeping room
finally they relinquish back to the tomb

as spirit's struggles mirror our lives
remember devotion is all that survives
our earthly flesh will melt away
but only ethereal love can stay

to attain peace in the heavenly abode
with mythic heroes you must have strode
journey amidst the noble in your worldly lands
then your goodness earns a place in the Creator's hands.

The Memorial

A memory haunts this sallow face
lined with weathered storms now lace
gossamer thin a specter in
these sacred grounds walk my kin

a recollection of temporal joys
in childhood wanders boundless toys
but the wings fly fast fleeing the pure
turning to evil dissolving life's tour

the rapture of flesh turns to stone
when gazed upon by an ancient bone
the animal digs but cannot find
these skeletal remains of man's mind

a tablet inscribed sums up the breath
endured by beings before their death
a record of glory in hallowed halls
dwells forever in celestial balls

a valley is lulled by silent voices
unheard except by human choices
a lullaby sung by family throats
form our castle's protective moats

no blot will tarnish my tired paper
for the ink writes in invisible vapor
a sea of mist rises from the ground
hidden in clouds seldom found

to sunset shores I tip my crown
as I aim not to frown
so my feature's lines stay shallow
and my flames burn from the tallow

the memories return with my ghost
as I stand watch at my post
I join the trees as sentinels ready
an armed forest with branches steady

I speak in tongues of tepid men
who walk the earth in search of Zen
had they but links to my recollections
remembrances would give more ardent directions

the genes that tie in bows and knots
are the ones that always leave the spots
but faults wash clean in paradise's rain
as we honor our loved ones' gain

at this time of monuments I glide along
a tide of men and ghosts so strong
throngs of spirits crowd around
to hear the songs rising from the ground

they are pleased to receive our praise
as the sheep in their field graze
the grasses upon which we walk
are the shepherd's divining stalk

The valley is deep with lilies blooming
the shadows overpowering all consuming
but the scent is unearthly sweet and luring
and the beauty of love eternally enduring.

Chapter Two
Family Love and Memories

For My Father

Your tiny baby makes a fist
of its little moving hand
that reaches out to grab the land
it says I stretch my limbs
my toes wiggle to try and walk
and see if they can even talk

do they want to hold me up
so I can stand and be a man
then amble through the sun I ran
into leafy green forests
basking under the moss-covered tree
covering my naked curiosity

I grow tall in your shadow's width
I play with kites that sing your joy
and furry lions become my toy
I spring up high as an oak
as you direct me on the stages
of my life's many macrophages

I inscribe my lessons in the stone
hewn by your desires to savor
life's gustatory alluring flavor
you pass to me through your music
star light notes in the holy grail
as I walk on the beach with my sand pail

I collect the ancient seashells formed
from the envelope of the home
you made for me from the celestial dome
above our door are engraved your arms
waiting for me kept safe
until I no longer am a lost waif

wandering through byways long gone
of streets where our memories walked
you showed me how the Greek gods talked
to each other in the whispering pines
in the ocean waves crashing on shore
the wind speaks through braveries roar

as we amble down through the years
now grown and aging in lime
a drink of the Jinn enhances our time
the magic wand you implanted
waves a mirage woven in silk
that I drink heartily as mother's milk.

My Father's Jacket

On that final summer last united
I walked into your closet and sighted
your jacket of woven tweed
British made for a gentleman's need

for sheep's wool arrives in colors diverse
blueprints to follow your life's verse
your ardor for existence in many hues
a North Sea sunset that inspires your muse

a cultured reverie on a loom you weave
wearing the shadowy mood on your coat's sleeve
my buried face draws comfort from your scent
the tender musty fragrance of my deep lament

nostalgia emanates from all your apparel
your passion for memories in a devoted carol
the song of the pious fills the air you inspire
my life's sheath is your protective attire

the fragrance of your aftershave cologne
dwells in every closet, your clothing tenderly sewn
I hear your voice in all your raiment
a royal array is your holy payment.

Mother's Birthday Memorial

My love is a river burning with flame
that I give to you in your name
a mother's labor becomes a baby new
a sketch in her youth that she once drew

made from charcoal and strongest lead
colored in hues from autumn leave's bed
in golden oranges my landscape of steel
becomes my teeth's future meal

my smooth pink skin stretched on a loom
is soft as a feather duster broom
that sweeps away the age from my brow
and the sweat and toil that time will endow

your flesh sings sweetly in soft phrases
as I ascend to meet your gazes
then you rise up the steps coming in peace
a spirit's calm you release

into air an ethereal vapor
only thick as a piece of paper
upon which I write of days gone by
antiques vanished in the wind with a sigh

as it blows through the trees in blustery gusts
the start of the season of Autumnal rusts
my hourglass grows short upon the sands
the storm at sea moves clock's hands

eras run in sheets of rain
off my roof shingles of paved grain
your lullaby nourishes my lonely soul
on river avenues we would stroll

your birth was an offering given to man
created before earth's mineral plan
a tribute paid is a birth award
we are connected by the familial cord

my love is a stream flowing ever towards
the tributaries of your rewards
the body rests while the spirit works
the angels are God's celestial clerks

filling his orders for new lives
creating catacombs for His hives
the flesh withers upon the bough
fluttering to ground in a leafy, spreading vow

you caress me with your tender form
comforting me through life's varied storm
the painting my mother made of me
ferries me across the open sea

to glories joined with her hand
in the luminous dusk of my childhood land
I return to my labors in my new life
in a glowing absence of mortal strife.

Grief

You left behind
a playbill of "Midsummer Night's Dream"
to show me that fairies do exist
and meddle in men's every turn and twist
as they plot their nightly scheme
on the moonbeams that you divined

you wanted me to know
the glory of the pauper's stage
where pennies are thrown like roses at the stars
the beauty of the musical bars
written on your soul's page
before you disappeared into the universal flow

you wanted me to hold
your words written on old parchment wood
of oak trees where our memories join
and I sprang from your root's loin
where with you Apollo once stood
giving me his healing gold

I try to recover from your death
but still I hear your lungs expand
in every dust speck of this home
you settle like gold dust over my loam
as you touch me with your tender hand
building my brick house with your breath.

The Stage

I tore from your book a page
of the scripts you wrote for the stage
written the day you were born
when the world was in early morn

the drama given to you at birth
were the masks of a play's worth
the smile turned upside down
soon became tragedy's frown

the plays you wrote were pearls in a strand
each one a poem penned by your hand
the play seen from a seat on the aisle
your throne placed where you're never on trial

without an audience there is no melodrama
no applause to heed childhood's trauma
in this show that you composed
the rhythms of life while your body dozed

In a sphere where you are principal lead
you inscribed in stone men's every word and deed
laid at your feet are roses and praise
on you the actors concentrate their gaze

as I read your beautiful description
of your life in the oyster's encryption
the world's pearls were there for the taking
genes decoded by the life you were making

with pen in hand you captivate all sorts
painted in rhetoric life's many retorts
lauded as a most wise sage
a life well played on this earthly stage.

A Mother's Love

Sweet as a mother I
am yours in soft cloths with a sigh
of delight at my baby's first speech
as I to her the alphabet teach

I embrace my role
as my newly-acquired, fitted goal
like a dress needing tailoring to fit
I search for threads from my sewing kit

little suspenders hold you up
giggling and squiggling like a pup
your tiny frame yields to my touch
like a fluffy, feather pillow on your crib's hutch

I teach you sentences from the words
brought to me by the fairy bluebirds
as sentences into paragraphs run
transformed into stories about the sun

I tend to my children with care
with cotton I wipe your pliant skin bare
a gentle touch I fondle your fingers
the afterglow of a mother's glory lingers

you cannot know the deep joy
of bearing from your body a little girl or boy
an earthquake shakes your body into milk
so the infant can drink it smooth as silk

as the lava flows down from my nipples
in the lake of my heart the pebble ripples
into ever widening circles spreading out
erasing the words on my chalkboard of doubt

the slate gray of my noon
becomes the rise of my rolling hills moon
as I bond with my little one's frame
after we've chosen a suitable name

hope lays high within a parent's soul
that their child will achieve a great life's goal
an elf's tale of earthly riches
sewn into a pair of corduroy britches

my pride in you is a kernel of corn
grown in a husk tightly shorn
planted in open fields on the plains
harvested by your blood that of me remains

my veins run through your molded clay
formed by ancestral homes where we lay
under a garden of sunflowers turning to face
your liberation into an open, wide space

I cover you in a gossamer sail
traveling through hill and dale
as snow blankets the vast earth
I paint your purity in tomorrow's birth.

The Begotten

Yesterday
I forgot
who begat who
in the sailor's knot
that I tied for my tot
to the dismay
of my captain's crew

today
the interlock
signs the symbols
of the ticking clock
where laden ships dock
to disembark on the clay
where play the thumbs and thimbles

tomorrow
I remember
where I left my ship
beside my flaming ember
in frozen pond's December
wearing boots I borrow
on the sphere's edge tip

the eternal
circle Celtic
adorns the pages
where pagan priests kick
lambs from the salt lick
down into earth's core infernal
where write the magic mages.

The Brow

Such longing for you within my brow
between these furrows that I plow
sowed in rows upon the brink
till deep in earth the seedlings sink

this sadness then springs from the dirt
borne to build a life inert
propelled skyward as a rocket
placed into my necklace locket

you sing a song of somber yearning
a heart-shaped container learning
how to fill a dream with seeds
while playing joy upon the reeds

a mystery arrives unto my heirs
the gift of shores with distant stares
a sight of eyes peers from the glasses
a concave vision through mountain passes

sadness rides on a sea foam wave
like the ripples on a forehead grave
but wishes rise unto the top
riding crests of the linear crop

succession's line will continue
through every fibrous hollow and sinew
the chimera flies into the sun
'til his silhouette says he is done

my thirst for you in water's glass
shows your reflection in polished brass
the candlestick upon my table
binds you to my family's fable

your image grows in mirror's face
in between my eyebrow's space
I nurture the wax from holy candles
in the seeds my gardener handles

so I can sculpt you from the devout
and nevermore have to pout
but keep you always by my side
ensuring your wax has never dried

I pine for you within my brow
between these furrows that I plow
the buds now burst from earth's skin
rising tall shoots of joy within.

The Gift

This is the gift you gave to me
that came from a rift in the family
a present wrapped in the color of merle
inherited from your throne as you drank tea of grey
      earl

a present in lacy snowflakes falling
from heaven dissolves as they touch my earthly
      calling
as silent emanations drench my frame
in descent these drops distance a wintry immortal
      flame

the royal legacy from your loins begot
stands somnolent as my natural lot
the more we part into travels lone
a forked road transforms into a wishbone

pulled apart on each end
this calcified matter does not bend
nor see the wicked from the chaste afar
where lays the remains in my antique mason jar
a specter flows from your alms
as the north wind rises, the drifting sand calms.

Cut from the Same Cloth

We were cut from the same cloth
at sunrise when we shared our morning broth
the pattern of the shimmering weave
was the path I later took to grieve

we connect in colors of gold
autumn leaf veins traced from the same mold
upon trees of elm
used to construct our ship's stormy helm

we traveled as a pair through our lives
and deeply forested car drives
into the foothills through the tidal bay
moving each in our own body's clay

our souls spoke one tongue, our bodies a different
      speech
we could not bridge the huge chasm breech
our flesh spoke of experiences given
and by diverse desires we were driven

we ambled through time perceiving the same view
of early morning grass with fallen drops of dew
and saw the fairies play in the mountain trees
we felt on our faces the salty ocean breeze

this single fabric was split in two
so our atoms would rejoin in a future life anew
but coming in one size human's mortal genes
it must be altered for our day's numbered scenes

the cloth was cut by a master tailor's tools
only for use with karma's rules
he formed and shaped it to our frames
from bodies to souls only with different names

so that the material he made would fit
he bought a special sewing kit
we wear the magic cloth from our lives past
costumes rendered from a ship's billowing mast

where we sail once more to return for another
     round
trying not to lose what we once had found
we've journeyed before on this earthly trip
from our broth we taste of it in a small sip.

Chapter Three
Eternal Life and Renewal

Identity Search

Look at your face in a faceted glass
fragments, a million pieces with no more mass
shattered on the ground
shards of archeology in an ancient mound

so identity leaps from the past
a life reconstructed from a cast
from a caveman with ancient bones
buried in the time of iron age stones

the person we are is the people we've been
the sum is the total buried in tin
a box in the ground that we reveal
we finally find our family seal.

The Physique

The body is a mass of dense stolid matter
made from the clay of the earth's batter
baked in dough forming a basis
for mankind's homeostasis

the skeleton is the framework of our home
its hammered shingles make up our roof's dome
the wooden timbers are under our skin
so that we have strength deep within

we spring from summer's rich brown dirt
living cells from the ground inert
created into a sensitive whole
our bodies substance comes from this sphere's bowl.

The Moss

Loss
is a moss
that you wear
as your gentle hair
a soft green shawl
covering your shoulder's sprawl
an aging tree roots call

rebirth
leads to mirth
born of clay
from your ancient dismay
a worn clothing patch
salvaged from a glade's catch
a mushroom from a burgeoning batch

growing
you are sowing
a phoenix rise
on your horizon's size
an angler's bait of shrimp
to capture plankton's limp
and trespass in mires scrimp

peat
that you eat
from a bog
in night's former fog
becomes a fairy's suit
ransomed as lichen loot
reclaimed as spirit's fruit.

Resurrection

It is the day of resurrection
in the season of seed's protection
when plants come out of their sheaves
as trees sprout new green leaves

like a movie speeded up
searching for immortality's cup
time is on a roll
as soil turns into coal

when night turns into day
reversal comes into play
as the axis upon which we sit
like a piece of wood is split

the plan of my desire
is the child I wish to sire
in my tilled dirt field
hoping to have a yield

when the virgin vessel is found
upon it we expound
to the fountain of youth we deliver
Cupid's arrow and quiver

the daffodil shyly appears
the vanity of narcissus rears
like a stag upon its legs
leaps into mirror's kegs

into a liquid brew
arrives a vision of veins anew
as the embryo grows in formation
striated leaves begin the creation

dandelion wine is pressed
to serve to our special guest
as nature is the host
to serve to the holy ghost.

The Bones

I hear the bones that speak
on top of mountain's peak
like ancient signal codes
they point to former abodes

strange figures form in the sky
signs that lead us to rivers dry
and in their beds we find
the life that we left behind

the bones arrange in shapes
an alphabet through which we traipse
searching for our ancient burial grounds
fiercely protected by Hades' hounds

our bones to life return
their utterance from which we learn
they imprint their stamp on sacred soil
where they wait for centuries in raiment royal

the skeletons mutter and talk
of primeval forests with deer they stalk
heed the tales of these old bones
hidden in venerable mountain zones

they look to be revealed
like some cryptic letter tightly sealed
a language unfamiliar to flesh of mortals
can only be decoded by time portals.

Persistence

Amber chews
the gum it accrues
in a petrified oak
of vestige's soak
not wishing a fossil
on crowds a jostle
old forests drink traces
of sapling's embraces

former self
the shadow of elf
flies fast to remain
a future gain
but resin's long smolder
turns into time's holder
a cup held aloft
by earthen croft

flies trapped
in ancient amber mapped
rings in wood staffs
become sailor's graphs
frozen in an ocean
of ossified still emotion
charts through past time
to tomorrow's clime.

The Colors of Time

Suspend for me in stained glass designs
my heart's desire in mountainous mines
where minerals form into colored rocks
arms rounding the corners of eon's clocks

shadows grow long in gentle wintry snow
as deep in the valley grazes the doe
untouched by time transparent colors lay
masterpiece of the hills in light of midday

soon a glowing sunset the mountain's frame
the sky on fire like a dancing flame
while beneath the earth time stands still
in the air it moves swiftly at heaven's will

the color of morning is the blush on the rose
as the golden sun arises from his nightly doze
climbing high skyward at noon overhead
the world is revealed as if by the dead

a starkness informs every stain on the earth
illumination appears in all species at birth
as evening shades fall over rivers and streams
a tint of white stardust brings hope to our dreams

as autumn approaches towards the end of our days
the hues of our lives are in mountain's haze
we attempt to scale the towering age
but find instead an ancient sage

in spring arrives the character of lambs newborn
awaiting summer when they will be shorn
time flies over the ocean of our softly tinged view
stirring the winds that we long to renew.

Transformation

I want all things the way they used to be
never moving in their same place
just as the moon and sun remain in stability
forever occupying the same space

I want not to search for the stars
but have them stay in their like orb
for viewed from the passions of Jupiter and Mars
the span is hard to absorb

but change relentlessly will appear
should this union be embraced
like a massing of grey clouds in a stormy
      atmosphere
amidst a summer's drought with a cool drink laced

the horseman rides up on a white stallion
who paws the air with shoed feet
looking like a ghostly galleon
moving in the direction of the main fleet

gliding over the waters of my resistance
comes an army in revolution
taking form from my consistence
in the guise of my evolution.

Immortality

I danced past a child on the beach
a castle he was making of pure white sands
a fortress for his ancestors within reach
he had hair of snow combed in strands

the bar of minerals decomposed over time
a quartz rock was his fortress strong
made these walls of unchanging lime
shaped by the deva's alluring song

I mistook him for a holy being
surrounded by the wide-open air
then realized I was a specter seeing
shaped in a deity's underwater lair

for many years after I returned to those shores
hoping to find that same youth
naively believing he would record his lores
on an inerasable tablet of divinities truth

but never again did he reappear
my golden boy to my childhood tales
yet still I retain an undying flame's burn
for those hallowed coasts where my heart sets sail

now I stand in a desert of unquenchable thirsts
the crystalline sand beneath my feet
the clouds shaped in frozen bursts
the rain pouring from the waves of heat

I touch the sky with my invincible shape
a superman for my future ages
but find I was only an unseen empty drape
a collapsed amorphous mass made of many sages

these dunes blow in a ceaseless whirl
a storm of the hourglass minute by era
wishing I could once again be a little girl
and walk on the grassy soft green terra

still I age and grow like the weeds
knowing the hills lie just over the plains
within my sight I write my deeds
but the disappearing ink leaves many stains

I walk to the mountains on imperishable rock
a landslide could be my end
as I fade into a sunset from the celestial clock
I turn the corner round the immutable bend

I look behind at what I gave up
the woods and dells of my frolicking spring
I enter the fount of youth drunk from a cup
I see the radiant phoenix rising

I leave this sphere for greater lands
than I can see from where I now sit
the new view should have more helping hands
and a mightier love for a better fit

I do not know where I will go
in this undying new majestic city
but I carry with me my rake and hoe
to plant a new spirit without pity.

AUTHOR BIOGRAPHY

Sharon Arthur has a B.S. degree in therapeutic recreation and a B.F.A. degree in painting and printmaking. She had a successful 20-year career as an artist and a painter in oils on canvas, with a commercial fine art gallery in Duck, North Carolina.

She was a caregiver for her elderly parents for the past 10 years, until their passing. She began writing poetry after her father's death as an outlet for her grief. When her mother died, she began to write short stories as well. Both of her parents were professional writers, so she comes by her writing talent naturally. She feels her parents are helping her to write these poems—that their beautiful spirits still live through these words.

To contact Sharon Arthur
go to www.SharonArthurWriter.com

Look for her blog at
SharonArthurWriter.com/blog

This book is also available
as an eBook at your favorite
online retailer.

www.ingramcontent.com/pod-product-compliance
Lightning Source LLC
Chambersburg PA
CBHW022216090526
44584CB00012BB/802